KU-024-342

YOU'RE NICKED

ON THE BEAT
WITH FOOT OF THE YARD

There are a lot of things they don't tell you about villains: mega-villains like Adolf Hitler, nasty, cunning people like the power-mad Borgia family, vicious madmen like the Roman Emperor Caligula. If you come along with me, you'll be able to meet all these monsters and more.

The word 'villain' comes from the medieval word 'villein'. The villein was a peasant who was given land to grow things on, in exchange for having to do jobs for the lord.

WHAT IS A VILLAIN?

A villain is a really nasty piece of work. Villains cause trouble and they hurt people. Stay clear!

Some villains get to be so powerful that they're the ones who end up making the law. When that happens, things can get very unpleasant indeed. In these cases, people who break the law may not be villains at all – they could be the good guys.

WHAT DO VILLAINS DO?

They steal, murder, cheat and terrorise people. Sometimes they do it for the pleasure of being really nasty – that sort of villain can be the worst of all. Like Vlad the Impaler – who liked watching people being impaled. Like Jack the Ripper – who liked stabbing women to death. Like Caligula – the Roman Emperor who once burst out laughing at a dinner party and said to his guests: "It just occurred to me that I only have to give one nod and your throats will be cut" – and he meant it.

What they don't tell you about
Villains

Help!..

By Jim Hatfield

This book is dedicated to Dick
Turpin, the highwayman, who gave
the game away by writing too much.

Hodder
Children's
Books

a division of Hodder Headline plc

EVENING ALL! I'M CONSTABLE FOOT 'FOOT OF THE YARD' THEY CALL ME. I'M HERE TO TELL YOU ALL ABOUT VILLAINS AND THE TERRIBLE TRICKS THEY'VE GOT UP TO IN HISTORY. READ ON IF YOU DARE...

Copyright © Lazy Summer Books 1995

The right of Lazy Summer Books to be identified as the authors of the work has been asserted by them in accordance with the Copyright, Designs and Patents Act 1988.

Produced by Lazy Summer Books for Hodder Children's Books

Text by Jim Hatfield

Cover portrait: CH20857 the Emperor Vespian by Peter Paul Rubens, (1577-1640), Christie's, London Bridgeman Art Library, London

Published by Hodder Children's Books 1995

10 9 8 7 6 5 4 3 2 1

All rights reserved. No part of this publication may be reproduced, stored in a retrieval system, or transmitted, in any form or by any means, without the prior written permission of the publisher, nor be otherwise circulated in any form of binding or cover other than that in which it is published and without a similar condition being imposed on the subsequent purchaser.

ISBN 0340 63624 6

Hodder Children's Books
a Division of Hodder Headline plc
338 Euston Road
London NW1 3BH

Printed and bound by Cox & Wyman Ltd, Reading, Berks
A Catalogue record for this book is available from the British Library

CONTENTS

 Whenever you see this sign in the book it means there are some more details at the FOOT of the page, like here.

WHAT MAKES A VILLAIN?

Some people say that villains are born bad. Others say they become bad because of the way they were brought up. Some say that people simply choose to be bad, because they are greedy or selfish. Take your pick.

WHAT HAPPENS TO VILLAINS?

Some villains get rich and die peacefully in bed – but not many. Most villains have horrible lives and come to a sticky end. They may get rich quick but most lose it all. Hopefully they get caught, and when they're caught they get punished. Punishments in the past tended to be more severe than nowadays but much depends on the type of crime they have committed. Here are the main types of punishment, ancient and modern:

☹ Fines – you have to pay money.

☹ Service – you have to work for others.

☹ Prison – you are locked up.

☹ Corporal punishment – pain is inflicted on the body.

☹ Capital punishment – death.

Sometimes, a villain may suffer more than one kind of punishment for a crime. At the end of this book, there are heaps of nasty examples of villains being punished. Sometimes the punishment seems more villainous than the crime itself.

WHO WAS THE FIRST VILLAIN ?

The answer could be 666 – that's the number of the Devil in magic. Otherwise known as Satan, he is supposed to have disguised himself as a snake and tempted Eve to take a bite out of the apple in the Garden of Eden – thus starting villainy for all time.

If Eve hadn't bitten the apple and passed it to Adam they would have stayed good and they would never have had to leave the Garden of Eden, dressed in fig leaves. From that time on, according to the Bible, it's been villainy all they way, starting with Adam and Eve's two sons, Cain and Abel. Cain was the first murderer – he murdered Abel in a fit of jealousy, while Abel was looking after his sheep.

ORIGINAL SINNERS

A Quick Visit To The Ancient Villains

Let's take a look at some of my files. Our records go right back to earliest times and you can get a quick look at some of the tricks the villains of old got up to. Ready? Right, let us proceed in an orderly fashion...

Some crimes haven't changed much. Murder, robbery and theft are pretty much the same as they always have been, though today's knave may use modern technology. Some say that human nature never changes. What do you think?

PYRAMID THIEVES

CRIME: They stole the treasures which were were buried with Pharaohs and meant for use in the next world.

WHERE? Egypt.

WHEN? 3000 BC – AD 1900.

TYPE OF LOOT: Gold, ornaments, mummies, anything.

VICTIMS: Dead Pharaohs, priests, the gods.

WEAPONS: Clubs, knives.

TRICKS: Working with the official guards to find their way around the secret tunnels.

PUNISHMENT: Death, chopping off bits of the body, digging town ramparts, working in the Nubian gold mines. In modern times, archaeologists such as Howard Carter (who discovered the tomb of Tutankhamen) reopened the graves and carted the treasure off to museums in Europe and America – but nobody punished them.

Except it is a fact that many of the archaeologists who helped Carter died later of unusual diseases...

BIBLE BADDIES

CRIME:
The Hebrews believed that they were God's chosen people and that everything they did was punished or rewarded by him. Bible baddies were the people who strayed from God's wishes, by doing wrong or by not following God's commandments.

WHERE?
In Palestine, or in exile in Egypt or Babylon.

WHEN?
3000 BC – AD 100

HOW DO WE KNOW?
The great Hebrew religious leaders and teachers preached against wrongdoers, and it is all written down in the Bible.

TRICKS:
All kinds.

PUNISHMENT:
The wrath of God.

Hebrew News

Women's page

Jezebel falls from favour
70 BC

Queen Jezebel of Israel, foreign wife of King Ahab and worshipper of the false god Baal, has been pushed out of a window to her death by her attendants. Jezebel was suspected of plotting with husband Ahab to murder innocent citizen Naboth. When Naboth refused to sell his vineyard, Jezebel trumped up some charges of blasphemy, resulting in the stoning of Naboth and the theft of the vineyard.

Salome wins by a head
c. AD 30

John the Baptist has lost his head simply because King Herod's daughter Salome asked for it. Herod had John executed and gave Salome the head on a plate after she agreed to do one of her naughty dances. Herodias, Herod's wife, put Salome up to making the deal, because John had criticised her marriage to King Herod. Herodias is still married to Herod's brother Philip.

Delilah's ex topples temple
c. 1060 BC

Strongman Samson has been crushed to death by the temple he pulled down in order to kill a throng of Philistines, who had packed the temple to watch his strong-man act. This mass destruction follows Samson's blinding and imprisonment at the Philistines' hands.

Samson's capture by the Philistines followed his rash marriage to delicious Delilah, the fair Philistine filly. She chopped his hair off while he was sleeping, and so removed his strength. She put her people before her hunky husband.

Samson was rated a major villain by the Philistines because he had killed many of their people and stole the Gaza city gates. He once caught three hundred jackals and tied firebrands to their tails – then set them loose to burn down the Philistine grainfields.

Anyone else for a haircut ?

Hebrew News

Court report

Sharp judgement

c. 950 BC

King Solomon has scored a big hit as a judge. When two women were arguing recently over who was the mother of a baby, he ordered the baby to be cut in two. As the baby was about to be cut in half, one woman said that the other could have the baby. Solomon reckoned that she must be the real mother because of her concern for the baby and has let her keep the child.

False hair   c. 1750 BC

Jacob has tricked his blind father Isaac into giving him wealth which should have gone to his brother Esau. Esau is a hairy man but Jacob's skin is smooth as a baby's bottom. With the aid of his mother Rebekah, Jacob pretended to be Esau by wrapping lambs' wool around his arms. The trick has caused bad feeling and Jacob has left home to start the twelve tribes of Israel.

Jesus slams funny money

c. AD 30

A little known man called Jesus has thrown the money-changers out of the temple at Jerusalem. The money changers are well known villains. Because Roman coins are not allowed to be used inside the temple for collections, the money changers have been selling local coins for Roman money and robbing the worshippers by charging an unfair rate.

Wife stolen   c. 1000 BC

David, the great king of Judah and Israel, is not beyond a bit of jiggery-pokery. David's military commander was the Hittite called Uriah and David took a fancy to Uriah's beautiful wife Bathsheba.

To get the husband out of the way, David had him lead the battle against the Ammonites. Now Uriah has been killed and so David is free to marry Bathsheba.

CRUEL EMPERORS

The Romans had more than their fair share of ancient villains. And worst of all were some of their own emperors.

HOW TO DISPOSE OF A CRUEL EMPEROR

The best way to get rid of an unpopular ruler was to have him bumped off. The mighty Julius Caesar was stabbed 23 times on the Ides (15th) of March in 44 BC, just as he was on his way to the Senate to be crowned. His friend, Brutus, thought he was becoming too powerful.

ASSASSINATED EMPERORS:

Vitellus – paraded through Rome with a noose around his neck while the mob pelted him with dung. After being killed, his body was dragged on a hook and then thrown into the River Tiber.

Tiberius – smothered by a pillow in AD 37.

Commodus – strangled in his bath by his favourite wrestler.

Elagabalus – butchered in a toilet, dragged through the streets of Rome and dumped in the River Tiber.

Claudius – killed by his fourth wife Agrippina, who fed him poisonous mushrooms.

THE GLADIATORIAL GAMES
HAVING FUN WITH SLAVES AND CHRISTIANS

Emperors needed to keep the Roman mob happy, and they did it with two things – free bread and circuses. Roman circuses were not today's sort of cheery circus where clowns pour water down their trousers. They were more like slaughterhouses swilling with blood.

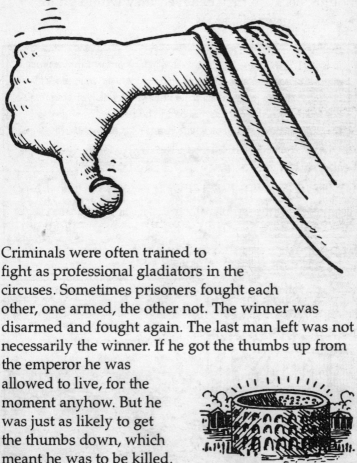

Criminals were often trained to fight as professional gladiators in the circuses. Sometimes prisoners fought each other, one armed, the other not. The winner was disarmed and fought again. The last man left was not necessarily the winner. If he got the thumbs up from the emperor he was allowed to live, for the moment anyhow. But he was just as likely to get the thumbs down, which meant he was to be killed.

MATCH OF THE DAY

Roman law, in the second century AD, said that everybody had to worship the emperor as a god. Christians refused to do this because they didn't think that the emperor was God. The penalty for refusing to worship the emperor was death, and Christians were sent to the circuses in large numbers. They were often quite cheerful about it though, because they believed they would go to heaven afterwards.

It is AD 177 in Lyons, an outpost of the Roman Empire. Forty-eight Christians are to be sacrificed to wild animals at the circus. Attalus is released from the fetter which chains him to his fellows and is paraded around the arena. He is naked but for a sign round his neck which reads 'Attalus the Christian'.

He is tied to a wooden stake called the column of shame, and the crowd, munching snacks, begins to buzz. Which beasts will they see today?

The Emperor Claudius loved the circus so much that there weren't enough Christians and prisoners of war to keep him happy. Romans had to be used as well.

On his orders, courts began condemning people to death for the most minor of offences, just to maintain a steady supply. Imagine dropping a sweet wrapper and being hauled off to feed the lions!

During the contests, Claudius ordered the statues of the gods and former emperors to be veiled, as a mark of respect. But there were so many contests that he had the statue of the God-Emperor Augustus removed, otherwise it would have been permanently veiled. The Emperor Caligula used to pretend that there was a shortage of meat to feed the beasts and ordered that the inmates of prisons be used as food.

KNAVES, KNIVES AND SWORDS

TAKE A LOOK AT THIS COLLECTION OF MEDIEVAL MUGGERS AND TUDOR BEGGARS

In the Middle Ages, it was often difficult to tell who was keeping the law and who was breaking it. Kings and knights were out to grab as much land as possible. So were bishops and monks. Crusader knights were out to gain booty from the Muslims. Merchants were out to make a profit from things like food, cloth and luxurious spices and silks. Robber bands would grab whatever they could from whoever they could.

Peasants had to stay put and work the land. If they didn't, they might become outlaws and join robber bands. Occasionally, they would revolt. The lords tried to keep them down.

DIG IT YOURSELF, KNIGHTY!

NASTY NOBLEMEN

CRIME: For hundreds of years, Europe was up for grabs, and kings and other nobles fought each other for control of the land. To do this they had to keep down the local population and fight off any other would-be rulers.

WHERE? Mainly Europe, but anywhere where there was farmland with peasants to provide the food, weapons and luxuries the rulers needed.

WHEN? AD 476 – 1600, from the break-up of the Roman Empire to the setting up of modern nations.

WHY WOULD NOBLES BEHAVE BADLY? To get more power. Some also liked to get famous for being cruel and tough, so their enemies would fear them.

WAS EVERYONE A VILLAIN? If you served your lord, your king and the Pope, you were thought to be good. If you disobeyed your king or lord, you were a traitor, and if you disobeyed the Pope, you were a heretic. Traitors and heretics could be executed.

AND ROBBER BANDS

CRIME:
Lots of people were shut out of medieval society. Perhaps they were criminals on the run, or discharged soldiers; they might be peasants who had fallen out with their local lord. They had no way of making a living so they took food and valuables whenever they could.

WHERE?
Anywhere they could find a safe location with a good food supply.

WHEN?
Robber bands flourished whenever kings were weak. For example, as long as England and Scotland were enemies, the border areas were full of robber bands. They lived in the bog areas and were called moss troopers. With modern armies and police forces, it is more difficult for robber bands to survive, but they can still be found in Latin America and Asia.

PUNISHMENT:
Usually death. Sometimes they were pardoned, in exchange for giving their fighting skills to the king.

ROBIN HOOD – WAS HE REAL?

Robin Hood is the most famous of all outlaws, yet almost nothing is known about who he was or what he did. He was said never to have harmed a woman, to have been loyal to the king, and to have robbed from the rich and given to the poor.

There was a real chap called Robin (or Robert) Hood (or Hod or Hode), and he was an outlaw for a while.

He was born around 1290, and his father,

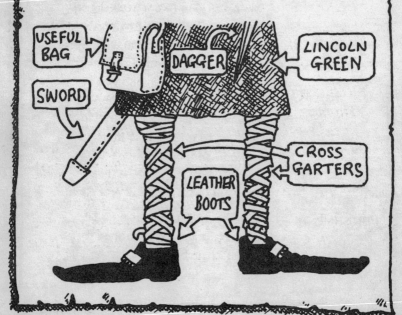

USEFUL BAG

DAGGER

LINCOLN GREEN

SWORD

CROSS GARTERS

LEATHER BOOTS

Adam Hood, was a forester in the service of the Earl of Warenne, a mighty lord who owned the manor of Wakefield in Yorkshire. In those days forests covered much of Britain, and Sherwood Forest joined up with Barnsdale Forest in Yorkshire. So you see, Robin Hood may have been a tough Yorkshireman!

Robin's, (or Robert's), landlord was Thomas, Earl of Lancaster, a great enemy of Edward II, who was king at that time. Thomas was eventually defeated by Edward II, and many of his supporters who were not captured would have become outlaws. It's very likely that Robin would have gone into hiding in Barnsdale Forest. As the Great North Road ran right through the forest, it made an ideal place for holding people up.

FOREST TIMES

Focus on outlaws

Bishop Davies jig

While travelling through Sherwood Forest, the Bishop of Hereford recently ordered the arrest of the outlaw Robin Hood, and his friends. But he found the tables turned against him. Robin, who had been roasting a deer, blew his horn. The Bishop was soon surrounded by outlaws dressed in Lincoln green. They made the bishop dance round a large oak tree and then demanded a ransom for his release. Further news of the Bishop is anxiously awaited in Hereford.

Outlaws in arrow contest

On a recent visit to Whitby Abbey on the east coast the outlaws Robin Hood and his friend, Little John, were asked to show off their skill at archery by the abbot. Shooting from the abbey roof, their arrows fell over a mile away. The fields where the arrows fell are to be named after the outlaws.

Outlaw in prison break-out

The notorius outlaw, Robin Hood, has been freed from imprisonment at Nottingham. His follower, Little John, led a daring rescue mission into the heart of the town and snatched their leader before he came to trial.

Outlaw gang pardoned

King Edward II has pardoned the outlaw band led by Robin Hood. The men in Lincoln green recently held up the king, and his knights, who had ventured into the forest disguised as monks, intending to capture the outlaws. Having discovered the identity of their royal captive, the outlaws bowed down and declared their loyalty. Edward has asked them to come and serve him at his royal court.

Outlaw chief dies

Having been taken ill at Kirklees Priory and being at death's door, the famous outlaw Robin Hood blew his horn, calling his friend Little John to his side. Summoning his last strength Robin shot an arrow through the window, asking John to bury him where it fell. Robin Hood's funeral takes place tomorrow.

 Little John was said to be a very big man. Legend tells that he was buried at Hathersgate in Derbyshire. In 1784 the site of his supposed grave in the churchyard was opened. Exceptionally large human bones were found in it.

PICKPOCKETS AND CUTPURSES

CRIME:
They stole from passers-by. Originally, clothes did not have pockets, and people carried money about in purses which they could tie around themselves or under their clothes. Children were especially suited to picking pockets. They were the right height, had small nimble fingers and were good at making their escape.

WHERE?
Any city street, preferably where there was a crowd of people staring at something.

WHEN?
From the Middle Ages and still going on.

WHAT LOOT?
Money. Handkerchiefs, made of silk or fine linen, could fetch a good price and there were pickpockets who specialised in stealing them.

TRICKS
Many. One trick was to roll a large grindstone along the pavement. As people leapt out of the way to avoid getting their toes mashed, they were robbed in the confusion.

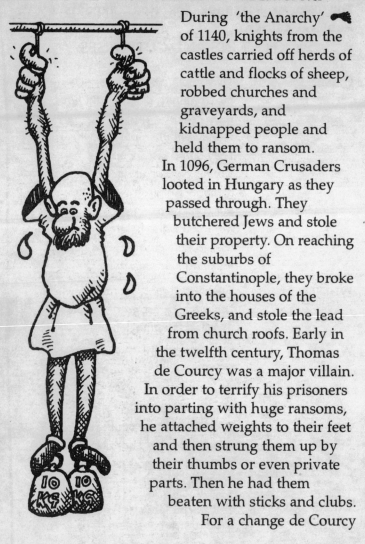

During 'the Anarchy' of 1140, knights from the castles carried off herds of cattle and flocks of sheep, robbed churches and graveyards, and kidnapped people and held them to ransom.

In 1096, German Crusaders looted in Hungary as they passed through. They butchered Jews and stole their property. On reaching the suburbs of Constantinople, they broke into the houses of the Greeks, and stole the lead from church roofs. Early in the twelfth century, Thomas de Courcy was a major villain. In order to terrify his prisoners into parting with huge ransoms, he attached weights to their feet and then strung them up by their thumbs or even private parts. Then he had them beaten with sticks and clubs. For a change de Courcy

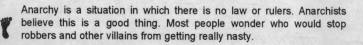

Anarchy is a situation in which there is no law or rulers. Anarchists believe this is a good thing. Most people wonder who would stop robbers and other villains from getting really nasty.

sometimes had the collarbones of his prisoners pierced. A cord was threaded through the holes, and the prisoners were marched off, six at a time, to his dungeons.

In 1303, stolen valuables that had belonged to Edward I of England kept turning up on the market stalls of London. Much of the loot was later found under the bed of Edward's palace keeper and more in the home of Richard Pudlicott, an ex-wool merchant's clerk who had fallen in with a bad crowd of monks. Many monks were implicated in the theft but Pudlicott agreed to take the rap in exchange for a light sentence. Unfortunately for him, the king did the dirty on him and Pudlicott was hanged. His skin, it is said, was spread across the chapel door as a warning to the monks.

ROGUES GALLERY:

THE REVOLTING WAT TYLER

In 1381 King Richard II's government slapped a new poll tax on the long-suffering English peasants. At the same time they passed a law to limit how much peasants could earn. The peasants revolted. Led by a Kent robber and small-time bandit, Wat Tyler, his mate Jack Straw, and renegade priest, John Ball, the peasant army marched on London. Many of them were out-of-work soldiers.

John Ball fired them up with a sermon that asked why there were different classes of people in society:

> *"When Adam delved and Eve span Who was then the gentleman?"*

In London, the rebels helped themselves to food and drink, and then got stuck into

A poll tax is a fixed tax for each person, no matter how rich or poor they are. 'Poll' means head.

a riot. Thirty-two of them died drunk in the Duke of Lancaster's wine cellar when his fabulously grand Savoy Palace burned down on top of them.

At the Tower of London they found three of Richard II's chief ministers and chopped their heads off. One of the ministers who lost his head was the Archbishop of Canterbury. The heads were spiked on pikes, carried through the city and displayed on London Bridge.

At a big meeting outside the walls of London, King Richard II promised to stop the new tax and offered pardons to the rioters. Lulled by Richard's promises and unhappy after Thomas Walworth, the Mayor of London, stabbed Tyler during the talks, the rebels gave up. Wat was drunk at the time.

Afterwards, King Richard broke all his promises. Wat and fifteen hundred others were all put to death. It's an old trick; promise first, punish later. Wat Tyler was a villain in the eyes of the nobles, but what do you think?

TUDOR BEGGARS

Two hundred years after the death of Robin Hood there were still thousands of men who had no place in settled villages and towns.

In 15th century France there was a beggars' mafia ruled by a King of the Beggars, to whom his subjects paid a yearly tax.

In England, King Henry VIII said everyone who could work had to work, even if no-one had any work for them to do. Then he shut down all the monasteries, where many people worked or at least were provided with food. After that the monks were also beggars of a kind. During periods of peace, too, there would be many ex-soldiers without work.

By Henry's time the law allowed for beggars to be whipped all the way back to their homes, no matter how long the journey. They could also be branded, made into slaves, or hanged.

FAKE BEGGARS

Short of execution there were many horrid punishments for beggars. At the very least, you were put into the stocks and pelted with rocks, rotten fish, dead rats and horse droppings. But because only able-bodied men and women were punished, beggars often pretended they had something wrong with them and, got up to all sorts of tricks to try and fool the authorities:

'Abraham men' were as sane as you or me. They pretended to be mad, claiming that they had just been released from Bedlam, a lunatic asylum.

'Cranks' chewed pieces of soap which made them foam at the mouth while they pretended to have an epileptic fit.

A 'Billy in the Bowl' propelled himself in a small cart and pretended to be paralysed. Really he was perfectly fit.

MOLL CUTPURSE, QUEEN OF CRIME

Mary Frith dressed as a man. She became famous as Moll Cutpurse. In those days purses were hung from the belt and could be cut free by thieves like Moll. Her fame spread when a popular play called 'The Roaring Girl' was written about her in 1611. The name may refer to the fact that she often appeared in court drunk.

Her fame probably saved her neck. She was captured many times, branded and imprisoned, yet lived to a ripe old age. From purse-cutting Moll changed to dealing in stolen property and she opened a high-class shop on Fleet Street from which she returned stolen goods to their owners for a fee.

Expanding still further, Moll ran a

forging operation and created a school of crime, passing on the art of pickpocketing and other crimes to new generations of London villains. In her fifties she turned to highway robbery. More for the fun of it than the cash!

During the Civil War between King Charles I and Parliament Moll became a Royalist supporter. Now turned sixty Moll held up and shot General Fairfax, the parliamentary commander-in-chief. Captured and sentenced to death, she bought her freedom by paying Fairfax £2,000. She continued her life of crime, now as a dealer in stolen goods, before dying of dropsy (an excess of fluids in the body), at the age of seventy-five.

In her will, Moll left twenty pounds for a party to celebrate the return of the monarchy.

CAN YOU PULL OFF AN A-MAZING ESCAPE?

TREASON AND TRAITORS

BETRAYING KING AND COUNTRY

In early times High Treason was the crime of plotting against the king, his wife or his eldest son. Treason used to be considered the most villainous of all crimes. Under Henry VIII, treason came to include almost anything that made the king unhappy. Petty treason, a minor form of villainy, covered wives who killed their husbands.

> Treason used to be considered the most villainous of all crimes.

To be hanged, beheaded or boiled in oil for ordinary crimes was bad enough, but high treason meant being butchered before death, that is: hanged, drawn and quartered. See the chapter Dismal Deaths for the full ghastly details. In 1238, a squire was caught breaking into the royal residence at Woodstock, Oxfordshire, where Henry III was staying. He planned to knife the king to death. To set an example, he was sentenced to be torn limb from limb by horses, then beheaded and

quartered. His limbs were to be
dragged through the city and
hung on a gibbet for
all to
see.

DEAD HEADS – MORE ON WHAT THEY DID

The heads of treacherous villains were displayed on a
pike or, in London's case, on the gatehouse of London
Bridge. The first to be so displayed was that of the
Scottish patriot William Wallace, executed in 1305. To
send the grim message of his defeat to his followers in
the north, his 'quarters' were put on display in
Scotland and the border areas at Newcastle, Berwick,
Perth and Stirling. But one person's villain may be
another person's hero. Wallace is a national hero in
Scotland.

When the Earl of Carlisle suffered a similar fate in
1323, his 'quarters' were displayed at Carlisle,
Newcastle upon Tyne, Shrewsbury and York. His
sister petitioned the king for the remains so that she
might bury them. Edward III let her have the bit from
York.

In 1535, John Fisher, Bishop of Rochester, was
executed for not accepting that Henry VIII was head of
the Church of England. Before his death, the Pope
promoted the bishop to cardinal and sent him the
cardinal's hat. On hearing this Henry joked "Before

God then, he shall wear it on his shoulders!" Fisher's head was displayed on London Bridge but was removed because it seemed not to decay but to look healthier with each passing day. Which is odd, because Fisher had always looked a bit deathly when he was alive.

THE GUNPOWDER PLOT

The gunpowder plot is the most famous secret plot in English history. How much do you know about it?

WHY DID IT HAPPEN?

In 1605, Roman Catholics were very unpopular in England. Many of them hated the Government. A group of Catholics decided to blow up the Houses of Parliament on its opening day. They chose that day because they knew King James I would be opening Parliament, and so they could blow up both King and Parliament together.

WHO WAS GUY FAWKES?

Guy (or Guido) Fawkes was a freelance Catholic soldier who had fought for the Spanish. The conspirators asked him to become their explosives expert.

How did they start?

Their first move was to rent a house next to the Palace of Westminster and begin digging a tunnel right under Parliament itself. For several weeks they tried to dig through eleven feet of solid stone. Then they discovered that they could rent a ground-floor room, vacated by a coal-merchant, which was right under the chamber of the House of Lords.

What was the explosive?

The cellar was filled with thirty-six barrels of gunpowder, covered with rocks and iron bars to increase the destruction from the explosion, and then hidden under a heap of coals and wooden sticks. The plan was to light a fifteen-minute fuse then board a boat for Flanders.

How were they caught?

It is now thought that the Government knew of the plot but waited until the night before so as to catch Fawkes red-handed. Certainly, the Government knew of an anonymous letter that was sent to a Catholic Member of Parliament, warning him to stay away.

Did Guy Fawkes talk?

As his fellow conspirators fled north, Fawkes had to withstand terrible torture for three days, before cracking and spilling the beans. Evidence of how he was tortured can be seen from his signature. He boldly signed 'Guido Fawkes' when he was first arrested, but by the end of his ordeal he could barely write a shaky 'G' and a line that tapered into nothing.

What happened to the conspirators?

Fawkes and seven other conspirators were tried at Westminster Hall. All were sentenced to be hanged, drawn and quartered. On 31st January, Fawkes met his fate in Old Palace Yard, Westminster. Still feeble from the torture, he could barely climb the scaffold steps.

Why bonfires on bonfire night?

The one thing they didn't do to him was burn him on a bonfire. Bonfires were lit as a celebration that king and country had been saved, and to this day they are burnt every year in Britain, together with an effigy of Guy Fawkes.

TORTURE TACTICS!

You've been caught in an act of treachery, and you're about to be tortured. The longer you hold out, the more pain there will be. On the other hand, your fellow conspirators need time to get away. Do you...?

..tell everything at once?

..hold out for two hours?

..hold out for two days?

..tell a pack of lies?

SCORE:

If you chose a) take 1 point for being honest about it. If you chose b) take 2 points for trying. For chosing c) take 3 points for courage. For d) take 4 points for cunning.

ROBBERS ON THE ROAD

THE BAD, THE UGLY AND THE HANDSOME

Highwaymen need coaches like vampires need blood. So until 1550 there were very few highwaymen about because there were only a few coaches and some horses and very slow carts on the roads.

It wasn't until 1657 that stage coaches made their appearance. Posters announced 'Flying Coaches' that travelled from London to Oxford at the unheard of average speed of three miles per hour! Coaches caught on in a big way. Most of the travellers were well-off. A long-distance coach from London to Chester could

cost a farm worker a whole week's wages. Things were looking up for highwaymen.

FOOTPADS

First off the mark were the footpads. These were not things that made your shoes comfy. They were highwaymen without horses. Hiding in the ditches of city streets and country lanes, they made a living snatching money and even handkerchiefs and wigs from passengers in passing coaches. To do this, they sometimes used a pole and hook. Spies were paid to keep an eye open for the big spenders in the taverns and inns.

LEMON AID

In the 1720s, a footpad band led by Obadiah Lemon progressed from pinching wigs to blocking the road with tree branches and robbing the coach passengers at pistol point.

SWINGING LONDON

It was a dangerous game. If caught, the robbers could swing at the end of a rope (hang). This made them more ruthless and determined to leave no witnesses who might identify them in court.

HIGHWAYMEN

A highwayman was a cut above a footpad. He was cool and he had a dashing, gentlemanly image. Highwaymen often wore masks and generally tried to avoid violence, as they needed to make a speedy getaway. Sometimes, however, they used violence to scare passengers or to get rid of someone who tried to stop them.

However, most highwaymen were really just brutal robbers who died young, twitching at the end of a rope. Their tarred corpses were left hanging from a gibbet as a warning to others.

DICK TURPIN – DASHING HERO OR DASTARDLY VILLAIN?

Dick Turpin is England's best-known highwayman. The story of dashingly handsome Dick's daring ride to York on his mare, Black Bess, in 1739 is what made him famous. Unfortunately none of it is true. It was all made up a hundred years later by a writer called Harrison Ainsworth.

Dick Turpin was in fact an ugly, bad-tempered sheep stealer and house-breaker, who tortured his victims. Black Bess never existed and he never made the famous ride to York. Turpin was a bit of a turnip. He accidentally shot dead his partner, Tom King, when the cave where they were living in Epping Forest was discovered.

UGH!

FANCY A TURNIP, BESS?

Turpin had a fortune of 200 guineas on his head - which means the authorities would pay £210 to anyone catching him. Turpin fled to Lincolnshire and then to Yorkshire. Instead of keeping his head down and living quietly on his loot, he shot a neighbour's cock and was hauled before the magistrates. A cock up? Or a cock down?

Using the name Palmer, Turpin wrote to his brother in Essex, to ask him to pay for the shot cock. Unluckily for him, the postman handling the letter had once

been Turpin's school teacher, and he recognised the handwriting. John Palmer, bird shooter, was discovered to be Dick Turpin, murderer and highwayman, and he was hanged in York, aged thirty-four.

THE END OF THE HIGHWAYMEN
HOW HIGHWAYMEN LOST THEIR WAY – AND THEIR JOBS

✤ Better roads meant more traffic which travelled faster – imagine holding up a Porsche travelling at 100 mph.

✤ The increase of Turnpike Trusts made highway robbery on toll roads a more expensive business. There were now more watchmen and toll keepers for the robbers to bribe.

✤ Police patrols and armed mail coaches all added to the problems of the poor, forgotten highwayman.

✤ Worst of all were the railways, which put an end to the coaching industry and the highwayman as well.

✤ The last execution for mounted highway robbery in England was at Taunton in 1831.

STOP PRESS

Highway robbery is making a come-back on continental motorways. Motorists are induced to stop by someone pretending to have had a break-down and needing help – then they are robbed.

Claude Duval

Claude Duval was hanged at the young age of twenty-seven. He was a Frenchman who worked as a highwayman in seventeenth-century England. Duval was a hit with the ladies. It was said that women dreamed of being robbed by so charming a robber so they could boast about it to their friends.

When a lady on one of the coaches he stopped began to play a flute, he danced with her. On another occasion, however, he tried to take a silver feeding bottle from a baby. The passengers had to remind him that he was supposed to be a gentleman.

Duval was arrested blind drunk in the Hole in the Wall tavern in London. He was visited in his death cell by dozens of high-born ladies who petitioned King Charles II for his release.

The king would have none of it though, and Duval went the way of most highwaymen, with a noose around his neck in 1670. So many people came to see his body afterwards that the streets were blocked for days and a judge had to order the body to be moved.

Sir John Popham took up highway robbery after he got married. He was a twenty-year-old ex-law student from Oxford University, so he knew what he was up to. He followed this career for ten years until Lady Popham persuaded him to return to the right side of the law. Despite his criminal past, which was common knowledge, Popham rose to become Lord Chief Justice and presided over the trials of Sir Walter Raleigh and Guy Fawkes.

Another noble highwayman was Gamaliel Ratsey who used to wear a horrible mask to scare his victims and who made those who had no cash pay by other means. He made an actor recite from Hamlet and a barber give him a free shave.

John Clavel was one of the few highwaymen to avoid the gallows. He specialised in holding up mail coaches in London. At his trial, he pleaded that he had "never struck or wounded any man, had never taken anything from their bodies or done them any violence." Although he was sentenced to death, he wrote to the king and was spared.

Robbed in verse

Walter Tracey once held up Ben Jonson, the poet and playwright, who spoke to him in verse. Not to be outdone, Tracey made up a poem of his own.

KNOW, BASE SLAVE, THAT I AM ONE OF THOSE CAN TAKE A PURSE AS WELL IN VERSE AS PROSE AND WHEN THOU ART DEAD, WRITE THIS UPON THY HEARSE;
'HERE LIES A POET WHO WAS ROBBED IN VERSE'

ER, NOT BAD - FOR A BEGINNER. REALLY VERY GOOD. BRILL- -IANT...

SIXTEEN-STRING JACK

Claude Duval was outdressed by flashy 'Sixteen-String' Jack Rann, so called for the silk strings attached to his buckskin breeches. Rann came to highway robbery from pick-pocketing, which didn't earn him enough to keep him in fine clothes. He spent a fortune on his togs and more money visiting the posh places in London where he could show them off. To pay off his debts he would simply rob another stage coach.

He boasted about his exploits but, though arrested six times in 1773, he was never convicted. This was probably because he always robbed in the scruffiest clothes he could find. In the court room, witnesses just couldn't believe that the dandy in the dock was the same man.

After his seventh arrest, Rann was so confident of getting off that he planned a party and invited seven lady friends to attend. But luck ran out on Rann. He was found guilty. The party went ahead anyway. Sixteen-String Jack went to the gallows in style in 1774 wearing a new pea-green suit and a ruffed shirt.

LONDON LOUTS

PETTY PILFERERS ON YOUR PAVEMENT

You think crime is bad today? You should have lived in London two or three hundred years ago. There were hardly any policemen, not much in the way of street lighting and the place was awash with gin. People could be dead touchy. The slightest insult might spark off a fight or a duel. It wasn't just the poor who caused the trouble.

Unruly gangs of aristocrats and their cronies roamed the streets. They had names like Mohocks, Scourers and Nickers, and went around smashing windows, attacking watchmen and robbing and raping for the fun of it. Some robbers, working in pairs, attacked pedestrians. One might blow smoke or throw pepper into the victim's eyes while the other picked his pocket.

THE GROTTY GARROTTERS

In the nineteenth century, mugging developed into the alarming crime of garrotting. A victim would find a rope, a cloth or a strong arm around the throat as he was strangled from behind – the grip tightening until he could neither shout nor breathe.

Other hands would roughly turn out a victim's pockets and seize any belongings, before he was thrown to the ground and kicked a couple of times to stop him raising the alarm. It was marvellously quick. The gang could be sure of grabbing whatever the victim was carrying without a struggle and leave him unable to give chase or call for help.

Garrotters became bolder. They came out of the alleyways and into the main streets among daytime crowds. They no longer waited for stray passers-by but picked out their victims. They robbed an MP between Parliament and his London club, and none of five constables on patrol nearby saw or heard a thing.

A few victims died, their throats crushed or sliced through by unskilled robbers. Newspapers seized upon this new terror, calling every mugging a garrotting and started a public panic. This probably helped the technique to spread beyond London. Anti-garrotting societies were formed and armed citizens took to the streets to defeat the menace, attacking and seizing any suspicious (usually quite innocent) men, and sometimes anti-garrotters themselves.

HOLD THAT MAN!

When the panic reached its height in 1863, more criminals were hanged than for a generation. Parliament passed the Garrotting Act. Convicts were to receive long prison sentences with flogging by instalments. Between the whippings they were allowed to rest, with the dread of the next whipping on their minds.

In the eighteenth and nineteenth centuries, many villains and their dastardly deeds had special names. Here are some examples:

MORNING SNEAKS

Waited for maidservants to air houses in the morning by opening windows and front doors, and sneaked in at the first opportunity.

LITTLE SNAKESMEN

Were young boys employed by housebreakers to gain entry by ways too small for a grown man.

THE RUM DRAG

A man pretends to be drunk and asks a wagoner for a lift on the back of his wagon while he sleeps it off. There he changes the parcel labels so they end up at a mate's house.

DINING ROOM POST

A man at the doorstep pretended to have a letter to deliver; the receiver (who had to pay, as this was before the age of the pre-paid post) went back to get the money while the thief sneaked in and stole what he could.

QUEER ROOSTERS

Criminals who listened for useful information in inns and other places while pretending to be asleep.

LIFTERS

Women who shoplifted using small hooks hidden in their hands.

THE KID LAY

Snatching money from children sent on errands. Children themselves were sometimes kidnapped in the street for sale to professional beggars, or if they were well-dressed, for the sake of their clothes.

RING DROPPING

The operator leaves a ring in the street and pretends to notice it at the same moment as his victim. Which of them should have it? The cheat pretends to think it is valuable but says the dupe can have it provided he gives him half of its estimated value. The latter, thinking he is on to a good thing, parts with the money only to find later that the ring is worthless. Still practised today!

THE RATTLING LAY

This involved jumping on slow-moving wagons in the street and throwing the parcels across to a partner in a faster-moving cart.

JONATHAN WILD, THIEF-TAKER

When goods were stolen, the thief took them to a receiver or 'fence', who lay at the heart of the underworld. The king of the eighteenth century fences was Jonathan Wild. He built up a regular clientele of criminals who brought him stolen goods. This enabled him to have a hold over them. Once they became unprofitable, Wild turned them in. He was thus also a kind of private detective or 'Thief-Taker General'.

Wild often returned stolen goods to their owners for a fee. It was safer that way. To have sold them would have made him an accessory to the theft.

Wild became so successful that he set up an office near the Old Bailey law courts. People who had been robbed came to

HAVE YOU LOST SOMETHING? PERHAPS I CAN HELP?

him. He insisted on an initial fee and a
list of the stolen goods. This way he could
check on whether the thieves were
cheating him.

As a thief-taker Wild sent sixty men to the
gallows, including the ace escaper Jack
Sheppard. By 1724 Wild had broken all
the major gangs in London and was in
complete control of the underworld. But
when 'Blueskin' Blake, one of his
accomplices, tried to cut his throat while
Wild was visiting him in prison, people
began to suspect that Wild was not the
honest man he professed to be.

He was found guilty of accepting a
reward for returning some stolen lace.
The law under which he was tried had
been passed in 1719 and was known as
'Jonathan Wild's Act'. On his way to be
hanged at Tyburn in 1725, he was pelted
with mud and stones.

In August 1898, the newspapers overflowed with the exploits of London gangs. Each district of the capital had its own gang.

THE VELVET CAP GANG

From Battersea, they walked along "pushing people off the pavement, knocking at shop doors and using filthy language". They were all armed with sticks and belts and wore velvet caps.

THE MOUTH ORGAN GANG

In another part of London, the papers reported:

"A gang of roughs, who were parading the roadway, shouting obscene language, playing mouth organs, and pushing people down."

THE LARRIKINS

There were gangs in Australia known as the 'Larrikins', who wore high-heeled boots with their bell-bottoms. They assaulted policemen, Chinese and women. They smashed windows, wrecked holiday resorts and spat on the steps of churches and on the congregation. Before the term Hooligan was used, young English ruffians were known as 'London Larrikins'

THE PEAKY BLINDERS

From Birmingham, wore bell-bottom trousers, neck scarf, heavy belt, peaked cap and short cropped hair with a donkey fringe.

Hooligans

The word 'hooligan' originally had nothing to do with football. It is said to be the name of an Irish family of brawlers who settled in nineteenth-century London. At that time there was a lot of hostility between the English and Irish immigrants brought over to build the railways. It was useful to blame the Irish for the troubles. This was also a reputation that the Irish had in New York, Chicago and other American cities.

Wooden-legged ruffian

In 1898 a 'wooden-legged ruffian' kicked a policeman with his wooden leg. In the struggle, the policeman unscrewed the wooden leg as he wrestled the ruffian to the ground. A crowd threw pepper at the police, causing such a commotion that it took twelve constables to get the prisoner to the police station.

GANGS AND GANGSTERS

CRIMINALS WHO JOIN THE CLUB

There are gangs and gangs. Perhaps there's a gang in your school? It's where most of the stupid people end up because they're frightened of being on their own. But gangs can be very dangerous.

ROMAN ROUGHS

Julius Caesar had a gang. In 53 BC, he and his mate, General Pompey, fell out. So Julius asked Rome's richest citizen Crassus (the name means 'thick') to put up the money to hire a gang to do his dirty work. But Pompey had ideas and a gang of his own. Pompey's gang were ex-gladiators, and more than a match for Caesar's lot. The two gangs fought it out until the Forum ran with blood and the River Tiber was choked with corpses.

Jesse James – Pioneer Of Train Robberies

The James gang, led by Jesse James and his brother Frank, were bank robbers. They also robbed trains. In fact, Jesse James pioneered train robberies in 1873. This upset the Pinkerton Detective Agency who were responsible for security on the railroads. They sent their men after Jesse.

Catching one of the Agency's men, Jesse hanged him from a tree with a note which read "Compliments of the James Boys to the Pinkertons". The James gang won public sympathy when the Pinkertons dropped a grenade down their mother's chimney which exploded, killing a child and tearing off the mother's arm.

A reward of $10,000 was offered, which proved too great a temptation for Bob Ford, a former gang member. On 3rd April 1882, he paid a friendly visit to Jesse. As James turned to straighten a picture on the wall, Bob Ford shot him through the back of the head – perhaps Bob Ford was a greater villain than Jesse James.

THE GREAT TRAIN ROBBERS

Jesse James robbed trains in 1873. Ninety years later the idea was taken up by a London gang led by Bruce Reynolds. The gang included an assortment of London criminals and specialists like 'wheel man' Roy James, who was a successful racing driver.

At 3.03 am on 3rd August 1963, the gang stopped a Scotland-to-London mail train by rigging the signals at a small village fifty miles from London. While robbing the train, they coshed a guard on the head, resulting in his death a few years later.

They carefully counted the loot in a nearby farmhouse. Unfortunately for them they left their finger-prints everywhere – especially on a Monopoly board!

It was the biggest ever haul from a train robbery – two and a half million pounds – but the police had no problem picking up fourteen of the seventeen-strong gang. The only problem was that the missing three had the bulk of the loot. Two escaped from prison but all were eventually captured...

...except Ronnie Biggs. He went to Rio and then on to pop stardom with the 70s punk band, The Sex Pistols. He's still there.

THE DUMB DALTONS

The Dalton Gang tried to copy the James boys but they were just too stupid. Grattan, Emmett, Bob and Bill Dalton, and their partners Dick Broadwell and Bill Powers hated trains and set up as train  robbers. Getting tired of trains, on 5th October 1892, they decided to rob two banks at once in their own home town of Coffeyville, Kansas. The whole thing went wrong from the start:

- They looked ridiculous in their false moustaches and beards.

- The main street was being repaired, so they had to park their getaway horses half a block away.

- They hadn't planned a thing. While half of the gang were robbing one bank of $20,000, the rest were waiting for a time lock on the other bank's vault to work.

- They were recognised by their neighbours who opened fire on them in a haze of gunsmoke.

- When the gunsmoke cleared Robert Dalton and his brother Gratton lay dead.

Bill Dalton missed the raid. Brother Emmett was captured and served fourteen years in jail and when released headed for Hollywood where he advised on cowboy films.

NED KELLY

Ned Kelly and his gang were Australia's top villains. They were so famous that, despite being a murderer of policemen, Ned Kelly is now a national hero.

Ned was the son of an Irish pig rustler who was transported to Australia. As a bad teenager Ned stole horses, following in his father's footsteps.

After his mother was arrested and imprisoned for hitting a policeman on the head with a shovel, Ned, his brother Dan and two mates turned outlaw.

By 1878, they had killed three policemen in a shootout and a reward of £1000 was offered. This was doubled as the gang pulled off more bank robberies.

Ned was captured when the gang were cornered in the Glenrowan Inn. Ned tried to escape wearing a bizarre suit of armour made from melted-down ploughshares. Bullets bounced off it but the armour was awkward to run in. Police brought him down by shooting at his unprotected legs. Ned was hanged at Pentridge Gaol, Melbourne, in November 1880.

THE KRAY TWINS

Ronnie and Reggie Kray had a gang, known as 'The Firm', and were the kings of London's gangland in the mid 1960s. They made their money by threatening people and demanding money, as well as by other dastardly crimes, but they could be generous to their friends. They might never have been caught but for Ronnie's bad temper. Taunted by a rival gang member about being gay, Ronnie shot him dead with a bullet between the eyes. It was then Ronnie's turn to taunt his brother about never having killed a man. Reggie put that matter right by hacking Jack 'The Hat' McVitie to death with a carving knife.

The Krays were not nice to know and felt themselves to be above the law. The police were just waiting their chance. In 1968, sixty-eight of them raided a house where the terrible twins were staying. The twins were sentenced to serve at least thirty years in prison.

Ronnie died in jail in March 1995. Six Daimler limousines followed his funeral carriage drawn by six black horses. So many people attended the funeral service that it had to be relayed to the world outside on loud speakers. His brother Reggie is still serving his sentence in Broadmoor, a hospital for the criminally

SECRET SOCIETIES

You Don't Know Where They Are

Secret societies are the most terrifying of all gangs. You never know who they are or where they may strike.

Tongs

Tong was the name given to gangs of Chinese immigrants to the USA, who needed to protect themselves against other lawless Chinese as well as the white population.

As the number of Tong gangs grew, disputes developed, resulting in clashes between the Tongs. Hatchets and knives were the favoured weapons. This is where the expression 'hatchet man' comes from. In 1897, Chinese Tong leader 'Little Pete' was murdered in a San Francisco barber's chair. He only wanted a haircut, but they cut off his life instead.

Triads are Tong sects which are still very active today.

The term 'tong' means a hall or meeting place. It came to be used by the white population in the 1880s, to refer to the secret societies that were involved in opium trading, protection rackets or gambling.

HASHASHIN

The Hashashin were an Islamic sect of the eleventh to thirteenth centuries. The name means 'hashish smoker'. The Hashashin , (the word 'assassin' comes from the Hashashin), were young men who were kidnapped, then drugged and then taken to a palace run by the Old Man of the Mountains.

When they woke up they were plied with wine and beautiful women and told they were in paradise. Then they were drugged again and sent out on dangerous murder missions. They had no fear of death because they were told that if they were killed in the course of their mission they would return to paradise.

The Hashashin, or Assassins, set up strongholds all over Persia and Iraq, and later also operated in Syria. Their power only came to an end as their castles fell to the invading Mongol armies in the thirteenth century.

The Mafia

The Mafia is the world's number one criminal society. It probably started in the Middle Ages, as a secret society for fighting against foreign conquerors of the island of Sicily, such as the Saracens, Normans and Spaniards. Having dealt with the foreigners, the early Mafia turned against local landowners and soon became the only law on many estates. Mafia members demanded money from landlords in return for 'protecting' the crops – which really meant not destroying them.

Around the end of the nineteenth century, some Mafia members emigrated from Sicily to America and repeated their crimes in the New World. The American wing of the Mafia became known as the 'Cosa Nostra' or 'Our Thing', an old name for the Mafia which may date back to the Sicilian Vespers, a patriotic uprising against French rule on Sicily in 1282.

WARNING! Don't ask a Mafia member to be a godfather to your child at its christening. The Mafia is divided into 'families' with a 'Godfather' at the head of each one. He demands total obedience.

During Prohibition, from 1923 until 1933, when the sale of alcohol was banned in the USA, the Mafia grew strong by making illegal beer and liquor and selling it at high prices. By the early 1930s, the Mafia had wrested control of crime from rival Irish and Jewish gangs. The Mafia are still going.

THUGEES

Thugees enjoyed strangling people. They were members of a secret Indian cult who worshipped the goddess Kali and who were dedicated to killing for killing's sake. They strangled their victims and would cut off a bit of the victim's body to prove to their friends they'd done the murder. They often held respectable positions in Indian society and spent their month's holiday each year roaming the roads for likely victims. They never killed women, poets, oil-sellers or a man who had lost a hand or his nose. Thugee was practised from one end of India to the other. It claimed about 40,000 victims each year for over five hundred years. It was stamped out by the British. Many old thugees were sent to prison where they gave details about their activities...

LOVELY WEATHER FOR THE TIME OF YEAR

Thugees would join a group of travellers. A victim would be picked out. One of the gang would chat to him in a friendly way, to make sure that he was someone who would not

When the party was resting at a chosen spot, a secret code phrase "tombaku khao" (smoke some tobacco) would be spoken.

TOMBAKU KHAO

LOOK! A LITTLE BIRD!

Right on cue, members of the gang would point eagerly to some object in the sky or in a tree.

As the victim looked up, he was killed bloodlessly using a special scarf, made of strong yellow and white silk with a large knot at each end and a slip-knot between.

The victim would be robbed of whatever he had on him.

A bit of the body would be cut off to show to other thugs as proof that they had killed someone.

Another member would dig a grave with a secret digging-tool. The victim would be buried so cleverly that not even a jackal could find him.

AL CAPONE

Al Capone was a sharp-dressing big-time villain and Mafia leader. When young he was slashed across his left cheek while leader of the vicious teenage 'Five Points Gang' in Brooklyn, New York. Thereafter, enemies called him 'Scarface'. This always made him very angry. Those who knew him were careful to call him 'The Big Shot'.

Capone fought and killed his way to the top of the criminal world and, in 1925, he was given the multi-million dollar Chicago crime business by his boss Johnny Torrio.

In the 1920s the prohibition on alcohol was in full force. Capone liked to pretend that he was giving a public service. He once remarked, "Someone has to throw some liquor on that thirst. Why not me?" It made him an estimated $60 million to $120 million a year. All those dollars attracted rival gangs like bees to a honey-pot. An Irish gang tried several times to

kill him. Capone had the Irish leader Dion O'Bannion executed. Knowing that the Irish would seek revenge, Capone decided to teach the Irish and their new boss, 'Bugs' Moran, a lesson. He circulated a rumour that a shipment of liquor would be delivered to a garage on Saint Valentine's Day, 1929. Five of Moran's gang turned up to be met by Capone's men disguised as policemen. They lined the Irish gangsters up against the garage door and blasted them with machine guns. Over two hundred spent cartridge cases were found afterwards. Two bystanders were also killed in the hail of bullets.

Such was the terror of Capone that the police could not catch him for many years. Eventually in 1931, he was put in prison for not paying tax! By the time he was released in 1939 he was paralysed by syphilis – a nerve disease, and died miserably in 1947.

'LUCKY' LUCIANO

While Scarface built his evil empire in Chicago, another villain, the Sicilian 'Lucky' Luciano, did the same in New York City. He got his nickname because he always seemed to avoid trouble. He lived up to his name in 1929 when he was the victim of an assassination attempt. Despite being stabbed repeatedly with an icepick and having his throat slit, he survived.

Luciano became the criminal king of New York by killing his own boss and a rival. With other top villains in the city, he formed a hit squad of contract killers known as Murder Incorporated. They were responsible for over a thousand deaths in their first five years of operation. Fees ranged from $1000 to $5000. One killer is believed to have committed over five hundred contract murders.

The bodies were rarely found. Many are thought to have ended up in a 'concrete overcoat'. In other words, their bodies were cemented into bridges and other newly-built bits of the city, or were dropped, encased in concrete, into the river.

Ku klux klan

The Ku Klux Klan was a very nasty secret society based on racial hatred which took root in the southern United States. The name comes from the Greek word kyklos, meaning circle. The first Klan was set up as a social club in Tennessee in 1865. It quickly became a centre for Southern white opposition to black equality. Klan members dressed in robes and sheets to frighten superstitious black people and to disguise themselves from the authorities. Klansmen whipped and killed freed black men and their white supporters, and torched homes and farms during night-time raids.

The Klan was reborn in 1915 out of fears that America would be swamped by immigrants bringing social disorder. Membership peaked in the 1920s at four million. A burning cross was the symbol of the new Klan, and white-robed members took part in parades and night-time meetings all over America. Cowardly, racist killings of black people were common. The Klan still exists today.

THE CONCRETE SUIT PUZZLE

One day, a lump of concrete was found in the river with a pair of feet sticking out of it. The man had been shot at some time in the previous week. The police, led by Detective Pat Doughnut, worked out that the killer and his victim could be any of six gangsters. From the clues below, can you work out who killed who?

Spud Doyle would never hurt his friend Legs Pasta.

Frank Furter was alive and was in prison at the time.

Al Beano and Dutch Chese were interviewed later by police.

In any case, Dutch Cheese never uses a gun.

Joe Pizza can prove he was out of town.

Al Beano never met the victim.

ANSWER:

Legs Pasta killed Spud Doyle. The killer couldn't have been Frank Furter because he was in prison at the time. It wasn't Dutch Cheese because he never uses a gun. Joe Pizza has an alibi – so that rules him out. And Al Beano never met the victim – so it wasn't him. So the killer was either Spud Doyle or Legs Pasta. The victim couldn't have been Frank Furter, (he was in prison). Al Beano and Dutch Cheese were interviewed by police – so neither of them was dead! And Joe Pizza is around to prove he was out of town – so he wasn't the victim. That leaves Spud Doyle and Legs Pasta as possible victims. Since we know that Spud Doyle would never hurt his friend Legs Pasta we can conclude that it was Legs Pasta who killed Spud Doyle. A bad choice of friends by Spud.

MAD, BAD, OR VERY BAD?

SPECIMEN A103

In the nineteenth century people called phrenologists thought villains were born bad and could be identified by bumps on their heads. Nowadays people tend to think villains are made bad by their upbringing.

DEALERS IN DEATH

GILLES DE RAIS – MAD OR BAD?

Gilles de Rais murdered three hundred children in fifteenth-century France. A brave soldier who fought alongside Joan of Arc against the English, de Rais believed that the blood of children would help his attempts to turn iron into gold.

POPE DOPE – MAD OR BAD?

Pope Alexander VI and his children Cesare and Lucretia Borgia were experts in the art of poisoning. On one occasion something went very wrong – they drank their own poison by mistake. The Pope died a week later of a violent fever. Only Cesare survived. He took an unusual bath which he thought would cure him. A live bull was tied down on its back and its stomach cut open while Cesare squatted inside the warm animal.

INHUMAN BEANS – MAD OR BAD?

Ever eaten a lot of beans? In Scotland until around 1600, a lot of Beans might have eaten you. The Beans were a gang of forty-eight cave-dwelling savages, led by Sawney Bean. They robbed, killed and ate about 1,000 people. Because they behaved like wild animals, they were treated as such when they were caught! The men had their arms and legs chopped off and were left to bleed to death. The women were forced to watch this before they themselves were burnt to death.

LIZZIE BORDEN – MAD OR BAD?

In 1892 Lizzie Borden was released from police custody for lack of evidence against her, following enquiries into the suspicious deaths of her father and stepmother. Both bodies showed signs of poisoning with prussic acid before they were bludgeoned with an axe. She inherited half a million dollars. A children's rhyme goes:

> "Lizzy Borden took an axe
> And gave her mother twenty whacks;
> When she saw what she had done,
> She gave her father twenty-one."

DR CRIPPEN – MAD OR BAD?

One day in 1910 Dr Crippen's difficult wife Belle Elmore disappeared. Crippen said she had gone to America. Meanwhile a young woman called Ethel Le Neve moved in with him. After being questioned by police, Crippen and Le Neve left England by boat for America. Police searched the house again and found a part of Belle Elmore's body. On board ship, the SS Montrose, the captain received a wireless message giving their description. The captain recognised them, even though Ethel was dressed as a boy and they called themselves Mr Robinson and son. Dr Crippen and Ethel Le Neve were arrested aboard the SS Montrose as the ship neared Quebec and charged with murder.

BILLY THE KID – MAD OR BAD?

Billy the Kid – real name William Bonney – committed his first murder at the age of twelve. Altogether he killed more than twenty people: most of them in cold blood. In 1881, he was trapped by Sheriff Pat Garrett in New Mexico and shot dead. He was twenty-one.

JACK THE RIPPER – MAD OR BAD?

In Victorian times, Jack stalked the foggy and poorly lit streets of London's East End murdering prostitutes. In 1891 Jack killed his ninth victim, Carrotty Nell. Desperate to find the identity of the killer, police even tried to photograph the eyes of the victim in the belief that his image might be held in them. No one has ever found out who he was – he may even have been Queen Victoria's cousin, the Duke of Clarence.

ASSASSINS

Some people murder for political reasons. This is normally called assassination. Here are two famous political assassinations. Do you think the assassins were good, mad or just plain bad?

RAMON DEL RIO – GOOD, MAD OR BAD?

In 1940, exiled Russian Revolutionary leader Leon Trotsky was assassinated in Mexico City by Ramon del Rio, a supporter of Stalin, Trotsky's political enemy. Ramon got into Trotsky's heavily guarded apartment by asking to discuss a newspaper article. He then smashed Trotsky in the head with an ice pick. Del Rio was imprisoned until 1953 and then given a Czech passport and allowed to leave Mexico.

JOHN WILKES BOOTH – GOOD, MAD OR BAD?

In 1865, US President Abraham Lincoln was shot in the head at a Washington theatre by actor John Wilkes Booth. Booth was a supporter of the American South during the war which Lincoln had won for the North. He slipped into the President's theatre box during the play and shot him in the back of the head. Leaping onto the stage, he broke his leg, but managed to deliver one last speech before escaping. He was shot dead twelve days later in Virginia. It turned out to be Booth's third attempt at killing Lincoln.

TEN TERRIBLE TYRANTS

TOP OF THE VILE PILE

Throughout history there have been mega-villains: men and women whose crimes have been so enormous that they are in a class of their own. Here are ten tyrants who are all different, yet nearly everyone who came across them was scared stiff of them, with good reason. It's hard to choose which of them was nastiest.

HEROD THE GREAT 74-73 BC

The trouble is there were several Herods – most of them bad. They worked for the Roman Empire as rulers of Judea. You've already heard about Herod the Biblical Baddy, about the one who gave the head of John the Baptist to his daughter Salome. His father, Herod the Great, was even worse. At the time of Jesus' birth Herod the Great was told that a baby born near Bethlehem would grow up to seize the throne. Just to be on the safe side Herod ordered the massacre of all male infants under two years of age living near Bethlehem. Joseph and Mary, Jesus' parents, managed to escape to Egypt, taking the infant Jesus with them.

Killing children wasn't enough for this particular Herod. He also murdered members of his family and political opponents. He had many sons who wanted the throne and two of them were strangled to death on Herod's orders. Drowning, strangulation and stabbing seem to have been his favourite methods of murder. All in all, he altered his will six times, because of his changing family circumstances.

CALIGULA AD 12-41

Caligula was Emperor of Rome for four years, AD 37–41. Like many Roman emperors and their womenfolk, he was greedy and cruel. He was also mad. He thought he was a god and had his horse made into a Roman senator.

He described Rome as "a city of necks waiting for me to chop". It is said that he even cut open his pregnant wife and ate the foetus. People were terrified of him. Even his own bodyguards were not safe from his murderous ways, so one day they murdered him in a secret passage of the palace.

ATTILA THE HUN, DIED AD 453

The Hun leader, Attila, united a number of barbarian

 'Caligula' means little boot.

tribes together into one huge and terrifying horde. He was known as 'The Scourge of God' and attacked the Eastern Roman Empire, killing thousands of defenceless people and laying waste their lands.

Attila then turned his forces westward, sweeping across Germany and into Gaul (France) until he was stopped by a Roman army. Undaunted, Attila rebuilt his army in Hungary, then swept across the Alps into Italy, butchering the inhabitants and setting fire to crops and forests as he marched on Rome. Only lack of food stopped him short of the city.

Attila withdrew and was planning another campaign against Rome in AD 453 when he died. Deprived of his leadership, the barbarian army broke up. The Huns rode back into Asia and the people of Europe breathed a huge sigh of relief.

Genghis Khan c. 1162-1227

Genghis Khan united the wandering Mongolian tribes. His Mongol horsemen, like the Huns, were short, tough men who rode short, tough, shaggy horses. Genghis led his wild horsemen into China and captured Peking. He then headed west across the deserts and mountains of central Asia as far as the Black Sea, killing everyone who tried to stop him.

A favourite trick was to make mounds of human heads after he had massacred all the people in a city which failed to surrender.

In this way Genghis created an empire which stretched almost 7000 kilometres, from the shores of the Pacific Ocean nearly to Europe. He was a tyrannical ruler, but he also issued a code of laws, called the Yassa, with which he maintained law and order through his vast kingdom. Obey you, Genghis?
Yassa!

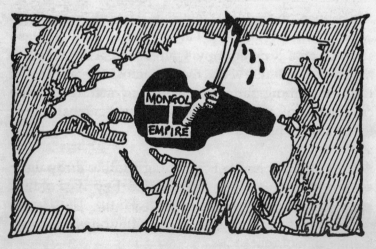

Torquemada was the boss of the terrible Spanish Inquisition. Queen Isabella of Spain had decided that everybody in Spain must become a Christian, including the large numbers of Muslims and Jews living in the country. "Convert or get out!" was her message.

In 1478, the queen appointed Torquemada, a Spanish monk, to enquire into the religion of everyone in Spain. Torquemada arrested anyone whom he suspected of heresy, witchcraft or any crimes against the Church of Rome.

Thousands of innocent and harmless people were clapped in prison and tortured. If they were found guilty at special courts or tribunals, they were burnt at the stake. The dreaded Inquisition also executed thousands of 'witches'.

DRACULA 15TH CENTURY

You may have heard of the vampire Count Dracula, who rose from his tomb and left his Transylvanian castle each night to feast on fresh blood. Dracula was dreamt up by a Victorian writer called Bram Stoker. But a real and even more dreadful Count Vlad Dracula (Dracula means the Devil or a Dragon), did live in what is now part of Romania in the fifteenth century. Some people have said that Count Vlad was a brave warrior who defended Christian Europe against fierce Turkish invaders. Perhaps. But Vlad was just as bloodthirsty as his fictional namesake.

Known as Vlad the Impaler, his favourite method of punishing anyone he disliked was to impale them on iron or wooden spikes. He killed thousands this way. He loved to eat his dinner with the screams of his victims ringing in his ears. Count Vlad once invited all the beggars and cripples in his kingdom to a banquet. He then sealed all the doors and windows of the hall and burnt them alive. When some Turkish messengers once failed to remove their turbans in his presence he had the turbans nailed to their heads.

IVAN THE TERRIBLE 1530-1584

Russia is an enormous land. In the sixteenth century, its people were cut off from each other by vast distances and long, dark, snow-bound winters. Most Russians were

serfs, virtually slaves, ruled over by cruel and ruthless nobles, called boyars. When he was just a teenager, the young ruler Ivan broke the power of the boyars by declaring himself the first Tsar of all Russia. He turned Russia into a great power by snatching more land and opening up trade with the outside world.

When his wife died, Ivan went mad. He believed that he was surrounded by people plotting against him, including the Bishop of Moscow whom he had strangled. He set up a secret police force and reigned through terror. Suspecting that some boyars in the old Russian city of Novgorod were plotting against him, he rode to the city with his troops, set fire to every building in the place and massacred the entire population.

He even struck down and killed his own son. It is said that this brought him to his senses and he died of remorse in 1584.

Tsar, or Czar, comes from the name of the Roman ruler, Caesar. Caesar probably comes from the Latin word caedere, to cut, because the founder member of Caesar's family, Scipio, was born by being cut from his mother's womb in an operation now known as a caesarian.

MAXIMILIAN ROBESPIERRE 1758-1794

Think of the French Revolution and you think of the guillotine. Think of all those heads rolling and you must think of Robespierre. Robespierre was one of the revolutionaries who demanded the execution of King Louis XVI and his Queen Marie Antoinette.

As head of the Committee of Public Safety, a kind of secret police force, Robespierre could arrest and execute almost anyone he chose. For almost a year, he was the virtual dictator of France, imprisoning and sending thousands to 'Madame Guillotine'.

The streets of Paris ran with blood during this terrible time, which was known as 'The Reign of Terror'. Finally his fellow revolutionary leaders began to fear for their own lives. Robespierre was arrested and lost his own head on the guillotine.

ADOLF HITLER 1889-1945

Adolf Hitler must be the worst villain ever. He believed that the Germans were a master race, superior to any other. So he tried to set up an all-powerful all-German super-state to last a thousand years. His armies smashed across Europe, and the conquered people were used in huge numbers as slave labour to run German factories.

Hitler, using his own brutal branch of the army called the SS, rounded up Jews, gypsies, and other minorities, and herded them into huge prison areas called concentration camps. He had many gassed, or shot, and many bodies were burnt in the ovens of concentration camps – camps where people were crowded together and used as slave labour until they died, or where they were just killed outright. Over six million Jews died in this holocaust and huge numbers of Poles, Serbs, Russians, Christians, communists and gypsies met the same fate. Adolf Hitler is the standard against which all other tyrants must be measured.

JOSEPH STALIN 1879-1953

Stalin became the Communist dictator of the USSR in 1924 and set about getting rid of his enemies. He dreamt of turning the country overnight into a modern industrial state.

He was responsible for the deaths of around thirty million peasants while he was building up a badly organised slave labour force. Writers, artists and composers were terrified of him. If anything in their works was critical of his regime he had them executed or sent to labour camps in the far, freezing wastes of Siberia.

Outside Russia, not many people knew what Stalin was up to and Stalin himself was portrayed as kindly 'Uncle Joe' with his pipe and big moustache. He ruled through a huge secret police force and executions without trial. After the Second World War, Stalin extended his terrible regime to the countries of eastern Europe, which his victorious Red Army had overrun. After his death in 1953, Stalin was gradually exposed for the monster that he was.

PAINFUL PUNISHMENTS

JUST READING ABOUT THEM HURTS!

Forget community service. Forget fines. Forget prison. Before the Norman Conquest, crime was simple and so was punishment. In Anglo-Saxon times murder was punished by death, unless the family of the victim would settle for cash. This was known as Wergild – lots for a noble victim down to nothing much for a peasant. The Normans introduced fixed payments for different types of injury. A farthing for the loss of a finger, more for a hand and so on.

MUTILATION

In the Middle Ages mutilation was all the rage. Ears were cut off, noses slit and hands were amputated. Criminals were branded on the forehead, hand or body. The letter showed their crime or position.

M for murderer	*X* for manslaughterer (killer)
V for vagabond	*S* for slave
T for thief	*F* for fraymaker or violent brawler

All these brands were applied immediately after sentencing. Some courtrooms had iron hoops set into the wall to pin down a criminal's hand. Sometimes the executioner could be bribed to apply the iron cold.

STREET PUNISHMENTS

EXPOSURE

In small towns and villages a simple punishment was to lead the troublemaker – a brawler, wife abuser, drunk or layabout – through the streets, shouting out their offences to the crowd along the way.

FLOGGING

More serious crimes might warrant a flogging 'at a cart's tail'. Tied to the back of a cart, the prisoner was paraded through the streets with their back exposed to the stick or whip.

THE STOCKS

Every parish had its stocks, usually close to the market place or crossroads. The offender sat with their feet trapped in holes cut through a wooden board, often with details of the offence shouted out to the crowd or written on a placard for all to see. They might be pelted with rotten vegetables, horse dung or dead rats.

THE PILLORY

Time in the pillory was much more dangerous than time in the stocks. Unable to protect his head or face from attack, a prisoner might be pelted with rocks or other sharp or heavy missiles. In 1751, two highwaymen who were exposed in the West Smithfield pillory, London, were so badly stoned that one died within half an hour and the other died soon afterwards. In 1777 Ann Morrow, who, disguised as a man, had married three different women, was so badly pelted that she lost the sight of both eyes. The writer Daniel Defoe was sentenced to the pillory at Temple Bar for writing rebellious pamphlets.  He had the sympathy of the crowd. In protest at his sentence they threw flowers instead.

THE SCOLD'S BRIDLE

Women who were thought to nag or gossip too much were called 'scolds' and might be forced to wear the 'Scold's Bridle' (known in Scotland as 'branks'). This was a metal mask with holes for eyes, nose and mouth. A metal tongue pressed onto the wearer's own tongue to prevent her from talking. In a nastier form, the bridle might have a sharp edge or vertical metal spikes which dug into the mouth.

THE DUCKING STOOL

Women accused of being scolds, witches and whores might be sentenced to the ducking stool, brought to England in the 16th century. This was a nasty punishment and would often result in the death of the victim. The victim might be brought naked to the stool in a wheel barrow or paraded around the town on a stool, and led to the river or deep pond and ducked in the water, repeatedly. Ducking was a great public spectacle. Some women drowned.

KICKED OUT!

OUTLAWRY

In Anglo-Saxon England a man could be declared an outlaw by a court and immediately have his land and all other possessions taken from him. He became a wandering fugitive with no rights. All law-abiding subjects were allowed to kill him and were expected to do so if they got the chance.

BANISHMENT

Banishment means being sent out of the country. Courts were allowed to banish rogues and vagabonds. Later they

could banish prisoners of war, petty thieves, fire-raisers, Quakers and even people who were just lazy!

TRANSPORTATION

During the reign of Charles II, some offenders were pardoned if the accused agreed to be sent, or transported, overseas. Transportees were sent at first to America, and then, after American Independence in 1776, to Australia. Sometimes transportation was for a period of seven years, sometimes for life.

GRISLY

PRISONS

Imprisonment was uncommon in medieval times, but medieval prisons were tough. Prison meant a slow death in chains. Unable to move, the prisoner felt intense and constant pain. Movement might be restricted by various cruel methods, such as hanging by the wrists, enclosing of the feet in a wooden block or underfloor burial with only head and wrists showing.

THE CLINK

The oldest purpose-built prison in London, probably in England, was built at Southwark in the twelfth century. This area, owned by the Bishop of Winchester, was popular for its brothels or 'stews', and was known as 'the Clink'. Later the name Clink was linked to other prisons.

The Tower of London

The Tower of London was sometimes used as a prison. It is riddled with cells and pits. One is just four feet square and nine feet high, which made it impossible to lie down. There in the pitch darkness, the prisoner could only crouch on the damp earth floor, cold, hungry and miserable, listening to the squeaking of the rats.

Tudor prisons

Treatment of villains in the 1500s was no better. The cells contained stocks and racks for stretching. One picture of the time shows a bishop suspended by an iron neckband, which just lets his toes touch the ground. It shows beds which were just pads of straw with a rotting bed-cover infested with lice and ticks. The toilet was near the bed and the whole place must have stunk.

Keepers used to run the prisons as a business. For the wealthiest, a place might be found in the keeper's own house. In the prison itself the most expensive and the most comfortable cells were at the top, but the charges for each level were so high that a man might run through all his funds, as he sank from one level down to the next and the next, until he arrived at the bottom – the dirtiest.

NEWGATE

Once London's prisoners were kept in gatehouses in the city walls. Newgate is the most famous of all the London prisons. It took over from the gatehouses.

Newgate became the jail for the most serious villains, many of whom would be hanged. By 1783 it had taken over from Tyburn as the scene of executions. The hangings of the inmates of the fifteen condemned cells were held in the open space right outside the prison door. At least there wasn't far to walk.

Executions at Newgate could attract vast crowds. Often far too many came for the space available. In 1807 thirty people died in the crush, many more than died on the scaffold!

UNFREE FRENCH

The French have had their fair share of villains. Like other countries it was sometimes difficult to know if the greater villains were the men on the outside, like the revolutionary Robespierre, or those rotting inside prisons.

The most famous of French prisons was the Bastille. This huge prison, or castle, was stormed by a mob at the outbreak of the French Revolution in 1789. They expected to find it full of people falsely imprisoned and were suprised to find only seven old men inside.

After the French Revolution, France was led by Napoleon who went to war with Britain. Devil's

Island was a famous French penal colony off the coast of South America. It was so disease-ridden that to be sent there was really a death sentence. One prisoner named Gerardin pretended to have leprosy by cutting off his fingers, so he was moved to a nearby leper colony and then escaped to Brazil. Then he really did catch leprosy, so the Brazilians built him a small prison of his own.

Dartmoor prison was built in 1806 to house French prisoners of war. It is still in use for serious British offenders and is surrounded by wild bogs which have claimed the lives of many escapees. Napoleon himself was the most famous prisoner of his time. First he was held by the British on the Mediterranean island of Elba, but in 1815 he escaped. He raised an army but was beaten again at the Battle of Waterloo. Then he was sent to a much more remote island – St Helena in the Atlantic, where he died in 1821.

THE BRIDEWELL

Imprisonment was common in England from the sixteenth century – but not just for villains.

Hoping to help the poor through a course of hard labour and punishment, Edward VI ordered that the royal palace of Bridewell, built in 1520, be turned into a refuge and workhouse. By 1556, the first inmates were making nails, cleaning sewers and spinning yarn. Those who failed to work were beaten. Some were singled out for special treatment, however. Prostitutes and vagrants were giving a whipping on arrival. Twelve lashes for adults, six for juveniles.

Unlike other prisons, the Bridewell was new, clean and disciplined. As well as a ducking stool and stocks, it had a doctor and a school master. It was seen as so successful that every town was ordered to provide a local house of correction.

It was also a place of entertainment for the public. The public whipping of women was always an attraction. It was so popular that a special gallery was built to hold the spectators. Flogging continued until the chairman, Sir Thomas Middleton banged his gavel. The sufferers implored him to "Knock, Sir Thomas, knock," a cry that was shouted after him wherever he went.

THE HULKS

In eighteenth-century England, after American independence, convicts could no longer be deported to America. The British made space for them on old ships called hulks, moored near the coast. They were shipped ashore during the daytime, where prisoners as young as ten years old worked without pay at backbreaking jobs, surrounded by armed guards. At night they were returned to the ships.

Conditions in the crowded ships were squalid, food was bad and typhus and cholera – caught from lice and rats – were rampant.The hulks would fill up with water and so prisoners had to work treadmill pumps to keep the hulks afloat. This caused sweat sores and so the treadmill was called a 'cockchafer'. There was great bullying and violence among the prisoners. Many died.

Introduced in 1776 as a two-year stop-gap, the hulks remained in use for over eighty years.

MILLBANK PENITENTIARY

In 1825 in Auburn, New York, the Americans built a penitentiary, a new kind of prison in which it was hoped villains would feel penitent, or sorry, for what they had done. Each prisoner had a separate cell.

The Millbank Penitentiary in London was then built as the first English prison on the same model. It was a disaster. It was a crazy maze of corridors with angles every twenty yards, winding staircases, dark, damp passages, innumerable doors and gates. One warder, even after many years, still kept a piece of chalk to leave a trail so he could find his way back. There were one thousand individual cells where prisoners were kept in solitary confinement. It drove them mad. In 1830, it emerged that three small girls, two ten-year-olds and a seven-year-old, had each been held in solitary confinement for twelve months. Early penitentiaries were meant to be an improvement but they probably caused more suffering than any prisons before or since.

THINGS TO DO IN PRISON

Prison reformers were keen on hard labour for prisoners. The treadmill provided consistent, all-weather toil. At Coldbath Fields prison in London there were twenty-six mills. The prison was detested in criminal circles.

At Leicester Prison prisoners had to turn a crankhandle 14,000 times every day. They had to turn it 2,000 times to earn breakfast and 5,000 for dinner.

Picking rope fibres (oakum) apart was a common prison punishment. Rock-breaking was another famous prison punishment. In America, chain gangs were hired out to local firms. Prisoners worked on farms, built roads or dug ditches. Convicts transported to Australia cut trees, built roads and were hired out as servants.

JACK SHEPPARD

Jack Sheppard (1720-24) was a useless thief but an ace prison escaper. In 1724 he escaped from prison four times. In one escape he had to climb through a window and down a knotted sheet with his huge girlfriend, Edgeware Bess.

In July, he was caught pickpocketing and sentenced to death. Locked up in a condemned cell at Newgate, he escaped by digging through walls, picking locks and climbing rooftops.

Captured again for highway robbery, he was returned to Newgate. The guard was trebled but next morning Jack was gone, up the chimney. His chains lay on the cell floor. He was now a national hero. But the fame did not last long. Within a week he was back inside, and despite huge public support he was hanged at Tyburn in November, 1724. He was only twenty-two years old.

Two hundred thousand came to see him off. Even at the last Jack hoped to escape. Before the hanging, a small knife was found in his jacket, with which he hoped to cut the noose.

VILLAINS' TORTURE TABLE

NOT A CHAPTER FOR THE FAINT-HEARTED

If you're a villain, torture is a dreadful thing to experience. And if you're not a villain you're bound to confess anyway to stop the torture. Heads they win, tails you lose. Torture was not so much a punishment as a way of getting someone to confess to a crime or reveal the names of their accomplices.

HIPPOCRATES' SHOE

A common dungeon treatment was Hippocrates' Shoe, in which the victim's feet were chained into cold water until the flesh came away from the bones. The torture was devised by an ancient Sicilian tyrant called Hippocrates .

PRISON FORTE ET DURE...

Slow starvation, a torture known as 'prison forte et dure', was always a good way of getting prisoners to

---

 Not to be confused with Hippocrates the Greek 'father of medicine'. He would not have thought this shoe to be healthy.

talk. 'Forte et dure' means 'tough and hard'. Chained in a cold, dank cell, the prisoner was given bad bread with no water one day; then dirty water with no bread the next day.

PEINE FORTE ET DURE

This was slow starvation and being pressed with weights as well. A refinement was added to this in Elizabeth I's reign when a stone was placed under the victim's back, thus snapping the spine.

PRESSING...

Pressing involved crushing the victim's body beneath heavy weights. In one sad case at Nottingham in 1735 a man was pressed to death after he refused to make a statement to the court. Afterwards it was discovered that he was a deaf mute – he wasn't able to speak. Pressing was used as a capital punishment in Ireland for the last time in 1740. Matthew Ryan feigned dumbness and lunacy after being caught robbing on the highway. Despite his pleas to be hanged, he was pressed to death in Kilkenny market place.

THE DUKE OF EXETER'S DAUGHTER

The rack was introduced from the continent in 1420 by the Duke of Exeter, when he was Constable of the Tower of London. Victims on the rack were said to have been 'wedded to the Duke of Exeter's Daughter'.

The prisoner was laid on his or her back over a wooden frame with ankles and wrists tied to axles at each end. These were worked by levers which pulled the body apart. Shoulders, hips, elbows and knees were dislocated.

The ropes were held taut during questioning so that the pain could be sustained. If the racking was tight enough, blood would seep from the fingertips and toes.

An official Tudor rackmaster boasted that he had stretched the Jesuit martyr Alexander Briant "a good foot longer than God had made him".

SKEFFINGTON'S DAUGHTER

This is the opposite of the rack. It was introduced by Sir Leonard Skeffington in 1534. Squashed and bent double in an iron press, with sufficient pressure, the chest burst and blood flowed from the mouth and nostrils.

The advantage of this machine was its portability. Smaller than the rack and free-standing, it could be moved up winding staircases to other rooms in the Tower.

JOHN FIENNES

Pity poor Scottish schoolteacher John Fiennes. In 1591 he was accused of casting a spell to raise a storm at sea that would sink the ship taking King James to Denmark. They took wizardry seriously in those days.

To make him confess, he was tortured with the 'boots' (see opposite page). Out of his mind with pain, he 'confessed'. When he came to, however, the silly man changed his mind.

The angry, torturer pulled out Fiennes' fingernails with a pair of pincers and into the raw skin of each finger pushed two needles, right up to the head of each needle.

Crippled, stretched and mutilated, Fiennes was then burnt alive at the stake on Castle Hill in Edinburgh before a huge crowd.

THE TORTURE CATALOGUE: INGENEOUS INSTRUMENTS FOR TORTURE

1) THE BRAKES

This was an iron bridle designed to force out the victim's teeth, one tooth at a time, between questions. In the 13th century, a Bristol man defrauded King John and was fined £6,500. Protesting that he couldn't pay, he was sentenced to have one tooth removed each day until it was paid. A week was enough.

2) BOOTS

These were imported from France and used in Scotland during the sixteenth and seventeenth centuries. One variety of 'boots' was to sit the victim in a chair and splint both sides of his legs with wooden boards. Wooden wedges were hammered between the boards and the legs, compressing and crushing the bones. Another variety was to put iron boots onto the prisoner's feet and heat them up so that the feet roasted. This was done to John Hurley, an Irish priest in 1583.

3) THE SPANISH COLLAR

This was an iron band lined with short, sharp studs, which the victim wore for several weeks. It weighed about ten pounds and was used on highwaymen in many prisons in the eighteenth century.

4) FINGER TORTURES

The Spanish Inquisition was keen on finger tortures. These included pulling out fingernails with pincers and inserting needles under fingernails.

5) THUMBSCREWS

Comical names were given to thumbscrews, like Pilliwinks or Finniwinks, which disguise the excruciating pain they caused. The thumb was crushed within a metal screw device.

6) FINGER PILLORIES

These locked a prisoner's fingers in an L-shape from the second knuckle and were used in many churches to punish those who had caused disturbances during services.

7) BAMBOO SHOOTS

This was a fiendish Chinese torture. The victim was forced to swallow some bamboo shoots and drink a lot of water. The shoots grew through the stomach in a few days, causing terrible pain.

DISMAL DEATHS

HORRIBLE ENDS FOR HORRIBLE PEOPLE

All over the world some pretty villainous people have put a lot of thought into how to make death as unpleasant as possible..

BEHEADING

Throughout history, having your head cut off has been reserved for the nobility, for it was considered the most dignified way to die. Expressions like "You're for the chop!" and "You'll get it in the neck for this" come from this.

The axe used was known as the 'heading axe'. It was little more than an unwieldy chopper. The blade crushed rather than cut the neck bones. The victim bounced off the block as each blow shook the planks of the scaffold. The Executioner Jack Ketch took five blows to despatch the Duke of Monmouth in 1685, so he must have bounced around a fair bit.

Ketch was so brutal and inefficient that when Punch and Judy shows arrived from Italy, the hangman puppet was promptly christened Jack Ketch. Blocks were old chunks of oak but over the years they evolved a shape helpful to the axe man.

Head Lines

- Queen Anne Boleyn, a wife Henry VIII grew tired of, asked that a sword might be used for her beheading instead of an axe. A Frenchman was brought over to do the job. He was so accurate and swift that as he lifted the head, the Queen's eyes and lips were still moving in prayer.

- The French were good at this sort of thing. When Charles-Henri Sanson executed a nobleman by sword in 1766, he cut so cleanly that the severed head remained balanced on the upright body for several seconds. Sanson said, "Shake yourself. It's done."

- Not all French were so good. Amateurs were sometimes recruited to do the job. In 1629, one took twenty-nine strokes to remove the head of the Comte de Chalais.

✿ Heads of decapitated nobles were displayed on London Bridge. One German visitor in Elizabethan times counted no fewer than thirty heads on the gatehouse.

✿ After Sir Walter Raleigh's beheading in 1618, his head was shown on either side of the scaffold then put in a leather bag and taken away by Lady Raleigh. It was preserved by her in a case for twenty-nine years until her own death.

HANGING

The English public used to love a good hanging. They went to the hangings like people today go to football matches or the cinema. Most towns had a gallows but the best shows were to be found in London's West End. Tyburn, where Marble Arch now stands, was the top gallows for a period. Prisoners were brought by cart three miles from Newgate Prison through streets packed with spectators. The hangings were always well advertised. Street vendors and pickpockets did a roaring trade. After 1783 prisoners were executed just outside Newgate prison instead of at Tyburn.

In 1262, Ivetta de Bolsham was still alive twenty hours after being strung up. Impressed, the King pardoned her.

In 1571 Tyburn had a new gallows. Known as the Triple Tree, it could take up to twenty-four victims at once. In those days, victims were strung up while standing on the cart. The cart moved and they died of strangulation, a slow death.

Some hangmen were famous. John Hooper, appointed in 1728, was always cracking jokes and pulling faces. He was known as 'Jolly Jack' and the 'laughing hangman'. His victims didn't always see the joke.

Another popular hanging spot was Execution Dock on the Thames at Wapping. Here pirates and other seafaring miscreants were hanged. Up to three hundred pirates met their end here every year.

THE WHEEL

St Catherine is the patron saint of wheelwrights. This stems from her own execution in fourth-century Egypt. Sentenced to die on a spiked wheel by Roman Emperor Maxentius, the wheel broke and flying spikes damaged a lot of spectators.

BURNING

Heretics were people who did not follow the official Roman Catholic faith. They were burned at the stake by cruel and bigoted Roman Catholics, since it was felt that only the flames could cleanse their souls. It was risky to make fires close to buildings, so it became common to hold burnings on open ground. It was an especially nasty way to go. Slowly roasting and choking in the smoke might take hours.

Some executioners strangled their victims first, or tied a small bag of gunpowder around their necks to hurry things up and save them from the pain of burning. Green wood was good because victims suffocated in the smoke before the flames got them.

OTHER WAYS TO END IT ALL

The Romans had a liking for crucifixion. Victims' legs were often first broken to make them fit the upright part of the cross, and to help them die quickly.

The Chinese had a bad thing called 'Death by a Thousand Cuts'. The victim was skilfully flayed with thin bamboo canes or knives, gradually removing all the flesh. The executioner practised on a block of bean curd. Perfection was not reached until the curd, like thick custard, could be repeatedly hit without breaking the surface.

Another Chinese execution was beheading with a sharpened bamboo stick attached to a swinging log. This acted like a guillotine coming from the side.

How to hang, draw and quarter

Execution for treason (plotting against the government) was by hanging, drawing and quartering. It was quite a complicated process. This is how to do it.

Step 1   String victim up on a gallows until the victim is almost strangled

Step 2   Cut down before dead

Step 3   Make a long cut in the stomach

Step 4   Draw the intestines through the incision and burn them in front of the victim's eyes

Step 5   Sometimes cut out the heart and show it, dripping, to the crowd

Step 6   Cut off the head and hold it high proclaiming, "Behold the head of a traitor!"

Step 7   Cut the body into four with an axe and knife

Step 8   Plunge every bit of the body into a cauldron and boil lightly in water. The water should be heavily laced with salt and herbs to preserve the body parts and make them taste unpleasant to birds.

Step 9   Coat with hot pitch or tar to seal each section against the weather

Step 10   Put the traitor on show, four quarters in four different towns, in the market square or on the town gates

The body was divided or quartered because of the fear that treason would breed further treason, that the followers of a rebel would rise again to overthrow the Crown. It was also a common belief that the human body had to be whole for a person to enter the afterlife and in cutting up the traitor's body the authorities were destroying not only a mortal body but also the person's soul.

DROWNING

Drowning was a common way of executing women. If suspected of witchcraft, a woman was tied hand and foot and cast into a river or deep pond. If she floated, then she was guilty because the devil had helped her. If she drowned, then she was innocent. Dead but innocent. As late as 1734, a woman in Saxony was drowned together with a dog, a cat and a snake for the murder of her husband. Animals were drowned with 'witches' to show how low they had sunk.

THE GUILLOTINE

Hands up if you thought the guillotine was French. Well it was, but the idea had been around in England before the French gullotine was invented. A headchopping machine called the Halifax Maiden, or Gibbet, had been in use in the Yorkshire town of Halifax since 1286. The blade came down with such force that the victim's head flew into the air. In 1587 one such head gripped the apron of a passing horsewoman with its teeth. The Maiden was operated by pulling on a rope, which loosened a bolt. If the victim had been convicted for stealing an ox, a sheep, or any other sort of beast, the animal in question might be invited to pull on the rope.

Dr Guillotin perfected his design in 1792, in time for the executions of the aristocracy during the French Revolution. He improved the angle of the blade so that the head rolled off the block rather than flew. Louis XVI suggested some improvements which were soon to be tested out on his own head. The French went wild over it. Models were bought for children. Guillotine brooches and ear-rings were all the rage.

During the Terror which started in 1792, over 20,000

necks felt the blade. The executioner was the ace swordsman Charles-Henri Sanson. He was good. A head a minute, and that included strapping them to the board.

Working conditions were not good. Blood soaked the scaffold, making it difficult for the executioners to stand. It dripped between the boards so that metal netting had to be fixed to keep the dogs away. The blood ran in the gutters and it stank!

MODERN METHODS

Although capital punishment has been declared a cruel punishment by the United Nations, many countries still use it on their worst villains, and on political opponents. Some forms of capital punishment are very painful. Who are the villains – the prisoners, or the governments who execute them?

Some countries which still have the death penalty use old-fashioned methods of dispatching the wrong-doer – like beheading and hanging. In an attempt to make the process more humane some American states use these modern methods:

ELECTRIC CHAIR

The electric chair, nicknamed 'Old Smokey' or the 'Hot Squat', replaced hanging in New York State in 1888, and was quickly adopted by several other states.

GAS CHAMBER

The gas chamber was introduced in Nevada in 1924.

It is a small airtight room made of steel, with a plate glass observation window. The victim is strapped to a chair, and the room is filled with hydrogen cyanide gas (prussic acid).

INJECTIONS

Another modern form of execution used in some American states is injection with a lethal chemical.

ABOLITION OF THE DEATH PENALTY

There is a trend in the modern world for countries to abolish the death penalty. At the present time there are fifty-five countries in the world which have abolished the death penalty for all crimes. Ninety-seven countries retain the death penalty. Some countries only use it very occasionally for what they see as very serious crimes. One problem with the death penalty occurs when innocent people get executed. Someone who's been put in prison by mistake can be released later, but a dead person can't be brought back.

JUST LET ME FINISH THIS LAST CHAPTER.

GRAND QUIZ

That about rounds up our guide to villains and their villainous deeds throughout history. Now that you're an expert villain spotter you could test your knowledge with the Grand Quiz on the following pages.

QUIZ STARTS HERE...

1) Who was the first Bible villain?

a) God
b) Cain
c) The Devil

2) Who lost his head for a dance?

a) Herod
b) John the Baptist
c) Jack 'the Hat' McVitie

3) What was an Abraham man?

a) a Biblical baddie
b) a beggar pretending to be mad
c) a bank-robber called Abraham

4) What was Guido Fawkes

a) a Spanish tour operator
b) a member of the Sicilian mafia
c) Guy Fawkes' real name

5) What was a footpad

a) a highwayman who
robbed on foot
b) a type of inner sole
c) a beggar with amputated
feet

6) How did Dick Turpin get caught?

a) his horse, Black Bess broke into a turnip field
b) his handwriting was recognised
c) he was captured in Epping Forest with his partner,
Tom King

7) Who were the Daltons?

a) a very successful gang of
robbers
b) a very unsuccessful gang
of robbers
c) a ring of fraudsters
specialising in rare
pottery

8) What was Rum Drag?

a) a boring conversation with a drunk
b) a scheme for stealing parcels from waggons
c) a betting syndicate

9) What is a Tong?

a) half of a fireside implement
b) a quick-talking confidence trickster
c) a Chinese gangster

10) How long was a thuggee's scarf?

a) two metres
b) there's no such thing
c) seventy-six centimetres

11) Who was Billy the Kid

a) an American murderer
b) a young male goat
c) an evil prankster

12) What was wergild

a) a type of wolf
b) an association of medieval villains
c) compensation for a crime

ANSWERS:

12 – c, 91	8 – b, 54	4 – c, page 37
11 – a, 79	7 – b, 64	3 – b, page 31
10 – b, 71	6 – b, 45	2 – b, page 12
9 – c, 67	5 – a, page 42	1 – c, page 8

If you got eight or more right you count can yourself an expert on villainous deeds in history.

INDEX

Read On

See if you can get hold of these books from your local library or bookshop.

RACK, ROPE AND RED-HOT PINCERS: A HISTORY OF TORTURE AND ITS INSTRUMENTS, BY GEOFFREY ABBOTT (HEADLINE 1993)
We have ways of making you talk. Think of the worst possible torture then double it.

OLD-TIME PUNISHMENTS, BY WILLIAM ANDREWS (TABARD 1970)
Gruesome punishments from history.

GOOD CON GUIDE, BY J. H. BRENNAN (SPHERE 1978)
Would you buy the Eiffel Tower from a stranger? It's happened. Tips from the great con artists.

DETECTIVE'S HANDBOOK, BY ANNE CIVARDI (USBORNE 1979)
How to become a brilliant detective. Loads of pictures.

GUILTY, BY JIM HATFIELD
(WATTS – HORRIBLE HISTORIES – 1993).
One of the most brilliantly horrible histories of villainy ever written.

CRAZY CRIMES, BY RUPERT MATTHEWS (PAN 1990)
Not all crimes are successful. In fact, some are downright crazy.

TRULY, MADLY, DEADLY – THE OMNIBUS
BY JOHN DUNNING (ARROW 1993)
A huge compendium of every kind of villainy you could possibly think of.